THE LITTLE REFUGEE

Anh Do

and Suzanne Do

Illustrated by Bruce Whatley

ALLEN&UNWIN

For Xavier, Luc and Leon

I was born in a faraway country called Vietnam.
It's a crazy place – strange food, snakes in bottles,
five people squashed onto the back of one little motorbike!

My mum and dad were very poor, so we lived with
Mum's family...lots of them! There were fourteen people
living in a tiny three-room house.

Even though we were poor and the house was crowded,
I was happy because there were always lots
of people to play with me.

I didn't know there was a war going on. Outside our house,
in the jungles and in the villages of Vietnam, many people
were dying. Lots of them were soldiers, but some were
mothers and fathers, and some were even children.

My father and many of my uncles were in the war fighting alongside the Australian and American soldiers. After the war ended their lives were in great danger because they were on the losing side. My family decided to escape to another country. From now on we would be refugees.

Our family, together with some neighbours and friends, bought an old wooden fishing boat that stank of fish.

Very early one morning when it was still dark we crept out to our boat. Forty people crammed on board.

At first the sun beat down on us.

Then luckily clouds came and gave us shade.

But then the sky turned black and an angry storm arrived.
Giant waves crashed down on our little boat.

I was terrified but my mum hugged me tight and told me,
'Everything will be okay. Don't worry, it will be okay.'

Finally, the storm passed and the sun came out again.

Mum and Dad stood together looking at all the food and water that had been ruined by the sea.

'At least we are all still alive,' said Mum.

But we were hungry and thirsty.

The next morning we awoke to the sound of
my uncle shouting, 'A boat! I can see a boat!'

A fishing vessel was approaching. It pulled
up alongside us and the fishermen jumped
on board our boat.

'Sit down, all of you!' the leader shouted,
waving a gun.

These men were pirates.
They stole everything we had –
rings, bracelets, necklaces,
even people's gold teeth.

A pirate grabbed hold of a baby. He lifted up the baby and ripped open his nappy. A tiny slice of gold fell out. The pirate dangled the baby over the side of the boat, threatening to throw him in. My father screamed, 'We must save the child!'

All the scared, hungry people on our boat stood up ready to fight these pirates to save the baby's life.

The pirate changed his mind and tossed the child at his mother's feet. His life was spared. That baby was my brother, Khoa.

As the pirates were leaving, one of them felt
sorry for us, and threw us a bottle of water.
It wasn't much, but it saved our lives.

The next day was our fifth day at sea. We saw another boat. Luckily, it was a German cargo ship and we were rescued.

'Everything will be okay now,' said my mother.

'What a great country!' my parents said to each other
when we arrived in Australia.

Two nuns came to visit and gave us a
huge bag full of clothes. There were little
boys' clothes and also little girls' clothes.
My mum had two little boys, but she
was too polite to say anything.

The next day we were walking down the street
and an old lady stopped to say to Mum, 'What
a pretty little daughter you have!'

Mum looked down at my brother, Khoa, and smiled.
He was wearing a girl's dress!

Soon we found a house to live in and I started
going to school.

I tried hard at school because I knew that would make my
parents happy, but I was really miserable.

I couldn't speak English very well so I didn't understand
my teacher. I had different food to the other kids and
some of them laughed at me. I even looked different
because I didn't have the right school uniform. Uniforms
were expensive and my parents couldn't afford to buy the
right one.

Mum and Dad started their own sewing business so they
could make more money and buy us all the things we
needed for school. They bought three brand-new sewing
machines.

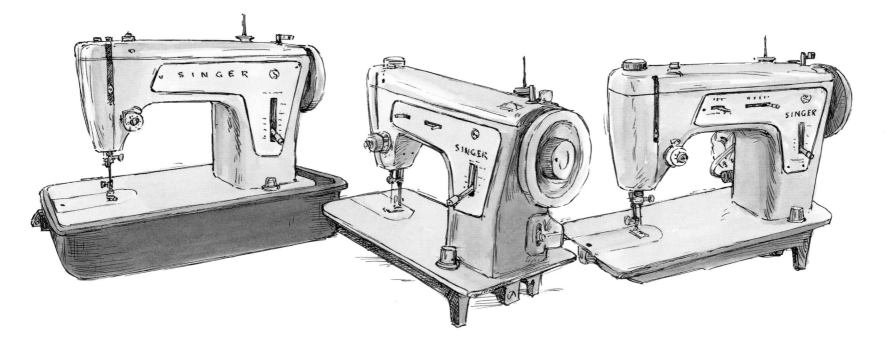

But then one morning Mum raced into the house yelling, 'Where are the machines? Who moved the sewing machines?'

The sewing machines were kept in a shed in our back yard. During the night someone had stolen them.

Mum was really quiet for a few days after that. One afternoon I heard her sobbing quietly to herself in the bathroom.

It made me very sad.

So I went and hid under my bed. Mum found me
and she climbed under there with me. We lay there
for a while.

'You know, Anh, I'm just a little bit sad now, but I'll be okay.
You must always have hope that things will be okay.
Remember when we were on the boat and that pirate threw
us a bottle of water? Even when things seem really terrible,
something good can come of it.'

I nodded my head, but I was doubtful.

Mum said, 'We are so lucky to be alive and living in this
beautiful country. There are many people much worse off
than us.'

Even though it was hard at first, I started to learn English properly. Each afternoon I would do all my homework lying on the floor among the sewing scraps. Slowly I started to do better at school, and began to make a few friends.

At the beginning of Year 3 a new kid started in my class.
His name was Angus and he had curly red hair and
a blue jacket with a patch on one elbow.

At morning tea he was sitting by himself eating a banana.
He looked very lonely. I remembered how lonely I used to be,
so I went over and asked if he wanted to play handball.

I played with him again the next day and the day after that.
Other boys started to ask if they could join in, and soon
we had a great handball competition.

At the end of Year 4 our school held a big prize-giving assembly. My parents never came to school functions because they were always working. But I begged Mum and Dad to take an afternoon off work so they could come and watch this assembly.

Throughout the awards I was praying that I would win one so that Mum and Dad would be proud of me.

The school principal reached the end of her list of awards. I didn't get one. I was so disappointed that I couldn't even look at my parents. They had taken a precious afternoon off work for nothing.

Then the principal said she was going to announce all the
class captains for next year. She read through her list and
everyone clapped politely for each of the new captains.
Finally, she reached the list for next year's Year 5.

'And the class captain for the 5 Blue class is ... Anh Do!'

I couldn't believe it! The kid who used to have no friends
and smelly lunch had become class captain!

As I walked towards the principal to shake hands,
I heard a big whoop from the audience. I looked down and
saw two people standing on their feet, clapping and cheering
loudly. It was Mum and Dad.

My eyes filled with tears as I looked at my parents'
smiling faces. I knew I had made them happy.

In spite of all the dangers and hardships they
had faced, Mum and Dad always told me
to have hope, and to believe that everything
would turn out okay in the end.

And they were right.
It did.

Anh Do grew up to become one of Australia's best-loved comedians. His book *The Happiest Refugee* is a national bestseller and was voted the 2011 Australian Book of the Year. Anh and his wife Suzanne are the proud parents of three sons.

Anh and Suzanne are donating 100 per cent of their profits from the sale of *The Little Refugee* to the Loreto Vietnam–Australia Program. Started by Loreto nun Sister Trish Franklin, the charity looks after extremely poor and disabled children in Vietnam.

First published in 2011

Allen & Unwin
83 Alexander Street
Crows Nest NSW 2065
Australia
Phone: (61 2) 8425 0100
Fax: (61 2) 9906 2218
Email: info@allenandunwin.com
Web: www.allenandunwin.com

A Cataloguing-in-Publication entry is available from
the National Library of Australia
www.trove.nla.gov.au

ISBN 978 1 74237 832 9

Teachers' notes available from www.allenandunwin.com

Cover and text design by Bruce Whatley and Sandra Nobes
Set in 20 pt Humanist by Tou-Can Design
Colour reproduction by Splitting Image, Clayton, Victoria
Printed in January 2014 for Phoenix Offset at Power Printing Factory,
Heyuan Hi-Tech Development Zone, Heyuan, Guangdong Province, People's Republic of China

7 9 10 8

Bruce Whatley is one of Australia's most respected author-illustrators, with over 50 books to his credit. Among his recent titles is the enormously successful and award-winning *Diary of a Wombat*, written by Jackie French.